Love
And
Death

By Sri Aurobindo

Copyright © 2021 Lamp of Trismegistus. All rights reserved. No part of this publication may be reproduced or transmitted in any form or by any means, electronic or mechanical, including photocopying, recording, or by any information storage and retrieval system, without permission in writing from Lamp of Trismegistus. Reviewers may quote brief passages.

ISBN: 978-1-63118-557-1

Esoteric Classics:
Eastern Studies

Other Books in this Series and Related Titles

Isha Upanishad and Commentary by Charles Johnston (978-1-63118-490-1)

Kena Upanishad and Commentary by Charles Johnston (978-1-63118-491-8)

Katha Upanishad and Commentary by Charles Johnston (978-1-63118-493-2)

Prashna Upanishad and Commentary by Charles Johnston (978-1-63118-494-9)

Mundaka Upanishad and Commentary by Charles Johnston (978-1-63118-496-3)

Mandukya Upanishad and Commentary by Charles Johnston (978-1-63118-497-0)

Yoga Sutras of Patanjali and Commentary (978-1-63118-536-6)

Atma Bodha & Tattva Bodha by Adi Shankara &c (978-1-63118-401-7)

The Crest-Jewel of Wisdom by Adi Shankara (978-1-63118-475-8)

The Book of Wisdom of Solomon by King Solomon (978-1-63118-502-1)

Catholicism, Yoga and Hinduism by Hartmann &c (978-1-63118-478-9)

Yoga, Hatha-Yoga and Raja-Yoga by Annie Besant (978-1-63118-476-5)

The Tree of Wisdom by Nagarjuna (978-1-63118-470-3)

The Path of Light: A Manual of Maha-Yana Buddhism (978-1-63118-471-0)

Buddhist Psalms by Shinran (978-1-63118-465-9)

Tao Te Ching & Commentary by Lao Tzu & C Johnston (978-1-63118-495-6)

The Hymns of Hermes by G. R. S. Mead (978-1-63118-405-5)

The Golden Verses of Pythagoras: Five Translations (978-1-63118-479-6)

Gnosis of the Mind by G. R. S. Mead (978-1-63118-408-6)

The Hymn of Jesus by G. R. S. Mead (978-1-63118-492-5)

The Book of the Watchers by Enoch (978-1-63118-416-1)

Audio versions are also available on Audible, Amazon and Apple

Other Books in this Series and Related Titles

The Use of Evil by Annie Besant (978-1-63118-532-8)

The Historic, Mythic and Mystic Christ by Annie Besant (978-1-63118-533-5)

Aurora of the Philosophers by Paracelsus (978-1-63118-507-6)

The Hidden Mysteries of Christianity by Annie Besant (978–1–63118–534–2)

Clairvoyance and Psychic Abilities by A Besant &c (978-1-63118-403-1)

The Feminine Occult by various authors (978-1-63118-711-7)

Alchemy in the Nineteenth Century by Helena P Blavatsky (978-1-63118-446-8)

Essays on the Esoteric Tradition of Karma by A Besant &c (978-1-63118-426-0)

Rosicrucian Rules, Secret Signs, Codes and Symbols by various (978-1-63118-488-8)

An Outline of Theosophy by C W Leadbeater (978-1-63118-452-9)

Paracelsus, the Four Elements and Their Spirits by M P Hall (978-1-63118-400-0)

The Secrets of Enoch by Enoch (978-1-63118-449-9)

Essays on Ancient Magic by Helena P Blavatsky (978-1-63118-535-9)

The Alchemical Catechism of Paracelsus by Paracelsus (978-1-63118-513-7)

Qabbalistic Teachings and the Tree of Life by M P Hall (978-1-63118-482-6)

History, Analysis and Secret Tradition of the Tarot by Hall &c (978-1-63118-445-1)

Crystal Vision Through Crystal Gazing by Frater Achad (978-1-63118-455-0)

Arcane Formulas or Mental Alchemy by W W Atkinson (978-1-63118-459-8)

The Machinery of the Mind by Dion Fortune (978-1-63118-451-2)

The A E Waite Reader: A Selection of Occult Essays (978-1-63118-515-1)

The Leadbeater Reader: A Selection of Occult Essays (978-1-63118-483-3)

Audio versions are also available on Audible, Amazon and Apple

INTRODUCTION

The word "esoteric" can be difficult to define. Esotericism in general can be seen less as a system of beliefs and more as a category, which encompasses numerous, different systems of beliefs. It's a bit of juxtaposition, since the word "esoteric" indicates something that few people know about, while the term itself broadly covers numerous philosophies, practices, areas of study and belief systems.

In a greater sense, Esotericism acts as a storehouse for secret knowledge, which is often considered ancient *(by tradition, if not by fact)*, passed down from generation to generation, in private. At various times in history, simply possessing the knowledge of some of these subjects, was considered illegal and a jailable offence, if discovered. This usually included such general topics as Alchemy, Pharmacology, Qabalah, Hermeticism, Occultism, Ceremonial Magic, Astrology, Divination, Rosicrucianism and so on. Collectively, these areas of study were often referred to as the esoteric sciences.

Sometimes, the outer garment of a subject isn't esoteric, while what is hidden beneath it, is. As an example, Freemasonry isn't necessarily esoteric by nature (at *least not anymore)*, but certain signs, passwords and handshakes given to the candidate during their initiation, are in fact, esoteric, in the sense that they are hidden from the general public.

Today, in the twenty-first century, such topics are readily available at bookstores across the country, and numerous mainsteam publishers offer beginners guides and coffee-table volumes on many of these subjects, intended for mass appeal. Books like *"The Secret"* have turned previously arcane topics into household knowledge. All that being the case, however, it isn't to say that there still aren't buried secrets to uncover, ancient wisdom being ignored and forgotten mysteries to be explored. In fact, it is often that we are only able to further our own studies by standing on the shoulders of these disappearing giants.

Lamp of Trismegistus is doing its part to help preserve humanity's esoteric history by making some of these classics available to those students who are seeking to unearth the knowledge of these ancient colossi.

So, be sure to check other titles from our *Esoteric Classics* series, as well as our *Occult Fiction, Theosophical Classics, Foundations of Freemasonry Series, Supernatural Fiction, Paranormal Research Series, Studies in Buddhism* and our *Christian Apocrypha Series*. You can also download the audio versions of most of these titles from Amazon, Apple or Audible, for learning on the go.

LOVE AND DEATH

In woodlands of the bright and early world,
When love was to himself yet new and warm
And stainless, played like morning with a flower
Ruru with his young bride Priyumvada.
Fresh-cheeked and dew-eyed white Priyumvada
Opened her budded heart of crimson bloom
To love, to Ruru; Ruru, a happy flood
Of passion round a lotus dancing thrilled,
Blinded with his soul's waves Priyumvada.
To him the earth was a bed for this sole flower,
To her all the world was filled with his embrace.
Wet with new rains the morning earth, released
From her fierce centuries and burning suns,
Lavished her breath in greenness; poignant flowers
Thronged all her eager breast, and her young arms
Cradled a childlike bounding life that played
And would not cease, nor ever weary grew
Of her bright promise; for all was joy and breeze
And perfume, colour and bloom and ardent rays
Of living, and delight desired the world.
Then Earth was quick and pregnant tamelessly;
A free and unwalled race possessed her plains
Whose hearts uncramped by bonds, whose unspoiled thoughts
At once replied to light. Foisoned the fields;
Lonely and rich the forests and the swaying
Of those unnumbered tops affected men
With thoughts to their vast music kin. Undammed
The virgin rivers moved towards the sea,
And mountains yet unseen and peoples vague

Winged young imagination like an eagle
To strange beauty remote. And Ruru felt
The sweetness of the early earth as sap
All through him, and short life an aeon made
By boundless possibility, and love,
Sweetest of all unfathomable love,
A glory untired. As a bright bird comes flying
From airy extravagance to his own home,
And breasts his mate, and feels her all his goal,
So from boon sunlight and the fresh chill wave
Which swirled and lapped between the slumbering fields,
From forest pools and wanderings mid leaves
Through emerald ever-new discoveries,
Mysterious hillsides ranged and buoyant-swift
Races with our wild brothers in the meads,
Came Ruru back to the white-bosomed girl,
Strong-winged to pleasure. She all fresh and new
Rose to him, and he plunged into her charm.
For neither to her honey and poignancy
Artlessly interchanged, nor any limit
To the sweet physical delight of her
He found. Her eyes like deep and infinite wells
Lured his attracted soul, and her touch thrilled
Not lightly, though so light; the joy prolonged
And sweetness of the lingering of her lips
Was every time a nectar of surprise
To her lover; her smooth-gleaming shoulder bared
In darkness of her hair showed jasmine-bright,
While her kissed bosom by rich tumults stirred
Was a moved sea that rocked beneath his heart,
Then when her lips had made him blind, soft siege
Of all her unseen body to his rule

Betrayed the ravishing realm of her white limbs,
An empire for the glory of a God.
He knew not whether he loved most her smile,
Her causeless tears or little angers swift,
Whether held wet against him from the bath
Among her kindred lotuses, her cheeks
Soft to his lips and dangerous happy breasts
That vanquished all his strength with their desire,
Meeting his absence with her sudden face,
Or when the leaf-hid bird at night complained
Near their wreathed arbour on the moonlit lake,
Sobbing delight out from her heart of bliss,
Or in his clasp of rapture laughing low
Of his close bosom bridal-glad and pleased
With passion and this fiery play of love,
Or breaking off like one who thinks of grief,
Wonderful melancholy in her eyes
Grown liquid and with wayward sorrow large,
Thus he in her found a warm world of sweets,
And lived of ecstasy secure, nor deemed
Any new hour could match that early bliss.
But Love has joys for spirits born divine
More bleeding-lovely than his thornless rose.
That day he had left, while yet the east was dark,
Rising, her bosom and into the river
Swam out, exulting in the sting and swift
Sharp-edged desire around his limbs, and sprang
Wet to the bank, and streamed into the wood.
As a young horse upon the pastures glad
Feels greensward and the wind along his mane
And arches as he goes his neck, so went
In an immense delight of youth the boy

And shook his locks, joy-crested. Boundlessly
He revelled in swift air of life, a creature
Of wide and vigorous morning. Far he strayed
Tempting for flower and fruit branches in heaven,
And plucked, and flung away, and brighter chose,
Seeking comparisons for her bloom; and followed
New streams, and touched new trees, and felt slow beauty
And leafy secret change; for the damp leaves,
Grey-green at first, grew pallid with the light
And warmed with consciousness of sunshine near;
Then the whole daylight wandered in, and made
Hard tracts of splendour, and enriched all hues.
But when a happy sheltered heat he felt
And heard contented voice of living things
Harmonious with the noon, he turned and swiftly
Went homeward yearning to Priyumvada,
And near his home emerging from green leaves
He laughed towards the sun: "O father Sun,"
He cried, "how good it is to live, to love!
Surely our joy shall never end, nor we
Grow old, but like bright rivers or pure winds
Sweetly continue, or revive with flowers,
Or live at least as long as senseless trees."
He dreamed, and said with a soft smile: "Lo, she!
And she will turn from me with angry tears
Her delicate face more beautiful than storm
Or rainy moonlight. I will follow her,
And soothe her heart with sovereign flatteries;
Or rather all tyranny exhaust and taste
The beauty of her anger like a fruit,
Vexing her soul with helplessness; then soften
Easily with quiet undenied demand

Of heart insisting upon heart; or else
Will reinvest her beauty bright with flowers,
Or with my hands her little feet persuade.
Then will her face be like a sudden dawn,
And flower compelled into reluctant smiles."
He had not ceased when he beheld her. She,
Tearing a jasmine bloom with waiting hands,
Stood drooping, petulant, but heard at once
His footsteps and before she was aware,
A sudden smile of exquisite delight
Leaped to her mouth, and a great blush of joy
Surprised her cheeks. She for a moment stood
Beautiful with her love before she died;
And he laughed towards her. With a pitiful cry
She paled; moaning, her stricken limbs collapsed.
But petrified, in awful dumb surprise,
He gazed; then waking with a bound was by her,
All panic expectation. As he came,
He saw a brilliant flash of coils evade
The sunlight, and with hateful gorgeous hood
Darted into green safety, hissing, death.
Voiceless he sank beside her and stretched out
His arms and desperately touched her face,
As if to attract her soul to live, and sought
Beseeching with his hands her bosom. O, she
Was warm, and cruel hope pierced him; but pale
As jasmines fading on a girl's sweet breast
Her cheek was, and forgot its perfect rose.
Her eyes that clung to sunlight yet, with pain
Were large and feebly round his neck her arms
She lifted and, desiring his pale cheek
Against her bosom, sobbed out piteously,

"Ah, love!" and stopped heart-broken; then, "O Love!
Alas the green dear home that I must leave
So early! I was so glad of love and kisses,
And thought that centuries would not exhaust
The deep embrace. And I have had so little
Of joy and the wild day and throbbing night,
Laughter, and tenderness, and strife and tears.
I have not numbered half the brilliant birds
In one green forest, nor am familiar grown
With sunrise and the progress of the eves,
Nor have with plaintive cries of birds made friends,
Cuckoo and rainlark and love-speak-to-me.
I have not learned the names of half the flowers
Around me; so few trees know me by my name;
Nor have I seen the stars so very often
That I should die. I feel a dreadful hand
Drawing me from the touch of thy warm limbs
Into some cold vague mist, and all black night
Descends towards me. I no more am thine,
But go I know not where, and see pale shapes
And gloomy countries and that terrible stream.
O Love, O Love, they take me from thee far,
And whether we shall find each other ever
In the wide dreadful territory of death,
I know not. Or thou wilt forget me quite,
And life compel thee into other arms.
Ah, come with me! I cannot bear to wander
In that cold cruel country all alone,
Helpless and terrified, or sob by streams
Denied sweet sunlight and by thee unloved."
Slower her voice came now, and over her cheek
Death paused; then, sobbing like a little child

Too early from her bounding pleasures called,
The lovely discontented spirit stole
From her warm body white. Over her leaned
Ruru, and waited for dead lips to move.
Still in the greenwood lay Priyumvada,
And Ruru rose not from her, but with eyes
Emptied of glory hung above his dead,
Only, without a word, without a tear.
Then the crowned wives of the great forest came,
They who had fed her from maternal breasts,
And grieved over the lovely body cold,
And bore it from him; nor did he entreat
One last look nor one kiss, nor yet denied
What he had loved so well. They the dead girl
Into some distant greenness bore away.

    But Ruru, while the stillness of the place
Remembered her, sat without voice. He heard
Through the great silence that was now his soul,
The forest sounds, a squirrel's leap through leaves,
The cheeping of a bird just overhead,
A peacock with his melancholy cry
Complaining far away, and tossings dim
And slight unnoticeable stir of trees.
But all these were to him like distant things
And he alone in his heart's void. And yet
No thought he had of her so lately lost,
Rather far pictures, trivial incidents
Of that old life before her delicate face
Had lived for him, dumbly distinct like thoughts
Of men that die, kept with long pomps his mind
Excluding the dead girl. So still he was,

The birds flashed by him with their swift small wings,
Fanning him. Then he moved, then rigorous
Memory through all his body shuddering
Awoke, and he looked up and knew the place,
And recognised greenness immutable,
And saw old trees and the same flowers still bloom.
He felt the bright indifference of earth
And all the lonely uselessness of pain.
Then lifting up the beauty of his brow
He spoke, with sorrow pale: "O grim cold Death!
But I will not like ordinary men
Satiate thee with cries, and falsely woo thee,
And make my grief thy theatre, who lie
Prostrate beneath thy thunderbolts and make
Night witness of their moans, shuddering and crying
When sudden memories pierce them like swords,
And often starting up as at a thought
Intolerable, pace a little, then
Sink down exhausted by brief agony.
O secrecy terrific, darkness vast,
At which we shudder! Somewhere, I know not where,
Somehow, I know not how, I shall confront
Thy gloom, tremendous spirit, and seize with hands
And prove what thou art and what man." He said,
And slowly to the forests wandered. There
Long months he travelled between grief and grief,
Reliving thoughts of her with every pace,
Measuring vast pain in his immortal mind.
And his heart cried in him as when a fire
Roars through wide forests and the branches cry
Burning towards heaven in torture glorious.
So burned, immense, his grief within him; he raised

His young pure face all solemnised with pain,
Voiceless. Then Fate was shaken, and the Gods
Grieved for him, of his silence grown afraid.
Therefore from peaks divine came flashing down
Immortal Agni and to the Uswuttha-tree
Cried in the Voice that slays the world: "O tree
That liftest thy enormous branches able
To shelter armies, more than armies now
Shelter, be famous, house a brilliant God.
For the grief grows in Ruru's breast up-piled,
As wrestles with its anguished barricades
In silence an impending flood, and Gods
Immortal grow afraid. For earth alarmed
Shudders to bear the curse lest her young life
Pale with eclipse and all-creating love
Be to mere pain condemned. Divert the wrath
Into thy boughs, Uswuttha—thou shalt be
My throne—glorious, though in eternal pain,
Yet worth much pain to harbour divine fire."
So ended the young pure destroyer's voice,
And the dumb god consented silently.
In the same noon came Ruru; his mind had paused,
Lured for a moment by soft wandering gleams
Into forgetfulness of pain; for thoughts
Gentle and near-eyed whispering memories
So sweetly came, his blind heart dreamed she lived.
Slow the Uswuttha-tree bent down its leaves,
And smote his cheek, and touched his heavy hair.
And Ruru turned illumined. For a moment,
One blissful moment he had felt 'twas she.
So had she often stolen up and touched
His curls with her enamoured fingers small,

Lingering, while the wind smote him with her hair
And her quick breath came to him like spring. Then he,
Turning, as one surprised with heaven, saw
Ready to his swift passionate grasp her bosom
And body sweet expecting his embrace.
Oh, now saw her not, but the guilty tree
Shrinking; then grief back with a double crown
Arose and stained his face with agony.
Nor silence he endured, but the dumb force
Ascetic and inherited, by sires
Fierce-musing earned, from the boy's bosom blazed.
"O Uswuttha-tree, wantonly who hast mocked
My anguish with the wind, but thou no more
Have joy of the cool wind nor green delight,
But live thy guilty leaves in fire, so long
As Aryan wheels by thy doomed shadow vast
Thunder to war, nor bless with cool wide waves
Lyric Saruswathi nations impure."
He spoke, and the vast tree groaned through its leaves,
Recognising its fate; then smouldered; lines
Of living fire rushed up the girth and hissed
Serpentine in the unconsuming leaves;
Last, all Hutashan in his chariot armed
Sprang on the boughs and blazed into the sky,
And wailing all the great tormented creature
Stood wide in agony; one half was green
And earthly, the other a weird brilliance
Filled with the speed and cry of endless flame.
But he, with the fierce rushing-out of power
Shaken and that strong grasp of anguish, flung
His hands out to the sun; "Priyumvada!"
He cried, and at that well-loved sound there dawned

With overwhelming sweetness miserable
Upon his mind the old delightful times
When he had called her by her liquid name,
Where the voice loved to linger. He remembered
The chompuc bushes where she turned away
Half-angered, and his speaking of her name
Masterfully as to a lovely slave
Rebellious who has erred; at that the slow
Yielding of her small head, and after a little
Her sliding towards him and beautiful
Propitiating body as she sank down
With timid graspings deprecatingly
In prostrate warm surrender, her flushed cheeks
Upon his feet and little touches soft;
Or her long name uttered beseechingly,
And the swift leap of all her body to him,
And eyes of large repentance, and the weight
Of her wild bosom and lips unsatisfied;
Or hourly call for little trivial needs,
Or sweet unneeded wanton summoning,
Daily appeal that never staled nor lost
Its sudden music, and her lovely speed,
Sedulous occupation left, quick-breathing,
With great glad eyes and eager parted lips;
Or in deep quiet moments murmuring
That name like a religion in her ear,
And her calm look compelled to ecstasy;
Or to the river luring her, or breathed
Over her dainty slumber, or secret sweet
Bridal outpantings of her broken name.
All these as rush unintermitting waves
Upon a swimmer overborne, broke on him

Relentless, things too happy to be endured,
Till faint with the recalled felicity
Low he moaned out: "O pale Priyumvada!
O dead fair flower! yet living to my grief!
But I could only slay the innocent tree,
Powerless when power should have been. Not such
Was Bhrigu from whose sacred strength I spring,
Nor Bhrigu's son, my father, when he blazed
Out from Puloma's side, and burning, blind,
Fell like a tree the ravisher unjust.
But I degenerate from such sires. O Death
That showest not thy face beneath the stars,
But comest masked, and on our dear ones seizing
Fearest to wrestle equally with love!
Nor from thy gloomy house any come back
To tell thy way. But O, if any strength
In lover's constancy to torture dwell
Earthward to force a helping god and such
Ascetic force be born of lover's pain,
Let my dumb pangs be heard. Whoe'er thou art,
O thou bright enemy of Death descend
And lead me to that portal dim. For I
Have burned in fires cruel as the fire
And lain upon a sharper couch than swords."
He ceased, and heaven thrilled, and the far blue
Quivered as with invisible downward wings.

    But Ruru passioned on, and came with eve
To secret grass and a green opening moist
In a cool lustre. Leaned upon a tree
That bathed in faery air and saw the sky
Through branches, and a single parrot loud

Screamed from its top, there stood a golden boy,
Half-naked, with bright limbs all beautiful—
Delicate they were, in sweetness absolute:
For every gleam and every soft strong curve
Magically compelled the eye, and smote
The heart to weakness. In his hands he swung
A bow—not such as human archers use:
For the string moved and murmured like many bees,
And nameless fragrance made the casual air
A peril. He on Ruru that fair face
Turned, and his steps with lovely gesture chained.
"Who art thou here, in forests wandering,
And thy young exquisite face is solemnised
With pain? Luxuriously the Gods have tortured
Thy heart to see such dreadful glorious beauty
Agonize in thy lips and brilliant eyes:
As tyrants in the fierceness of others' pangs
Joy and feel strong, clothing with brilliant fire,
Tyrants in Titan lands. Needs must her mouth
Have been pure honey and her bosom a charm,
Whom thou desirest seeing not the green
And common lovely sounds hast quite forgot."
And Ruru, mastered by the God, replied:
"I know thee by thy cruel beauty bright,
Kama, who makest many worlds one fire.
Ah, wherefore wilt thou ask of her to increase
The passion and regret? Thou knowest, great love!
Thy nymph her mother, if thou truly art he
And not a dream of my disastrous soul."
But with the thrilled eternal smile that makes
The spring, the lover of Rathi golden-limbed
Replied to Ruru, "Mortal, I am he;

I am that Madan who inform the stars
With lustre and on life's wide canvas fill
Pictures of light and shade, of joy and tears,
Make ordinary moments wonderful
And common speech a charm: knit life to life
With interfusions of opposing souls
And sudden meetings and slow sorceries:
Wing the boy bridegroom to that panting breast,
Smite Gods with mortal faces, dreadfully
Among great beautiful kings and watched by eyes
That burn, force on the virgin's fainting limbs
And drive her to the one face never seen,
The one breast meant eternally for her.
By me come wedded sweets, by me the wife's
Busy delight and passionate obedience,
And loving eager service never sated,
And happy lips, and worshipping soft eyes:
And mine the husband's hungry arms and use
Unwearying of old tender words and ways,
Joy of her hair, and silent pleasure felt
Of nearness to one dear familiar shape.
Nor only these, but many affections bright
And soft glad things cluster around my name.
I plant fraternal tender yearnings, make
The sister's sweet attractiveness and leap
Of heart towards imperious kindred blood,
And the young mother's passionate deep look,
Earth's high similitude of One not earth,
Teach filial heart-beats strong. These are my gifts
For which men praise me, these my glories calm:
But fiercer shafts I can, wild storms blown down
Shaking fixed minds and melting marble natures,

Tears and dumb bitterness and pain unpitied,
Racked thirsting jealousy and kind hearts made stone:
And in undisciplined huge souls I sow
Dire vengeance and impossible cruelties,
Cold lusts that linger and fierce fickleness,
The loves close kin to hate, brute violence
And mad insatiable longings pale,
And passion blind as death and deaf as swords.
O mortal, all deep-souled desires and all
Yearnings immense are mine, so much I can."
So as he spoke, his face grew wonderful
With vast suggestion, his human-seeming limbs
Brightened with a soft splendour: luminous hints
Of the concealed divinity transpired.
But soon with a slight discontented frown:
"So much I can, as even the great Gods learn.
Only with death I wrestle in vain, until
My passionate godhead all becomes a doubt.
Mortal, I am the light in stars, of flowers
The bloom, the nameless fragrance that pervades
Creation: but behind me, older than me,
He comes with night and cold tremendous shade.
Hard is the way to him, most hard to find,
Harder to tread, for perishable feet
Almost impossible. Yet, O fair youth,
If thou must needs go down, and thou art strong
In passion and in constancy, nor easy
The soul to slay that has survived such grief
Steel then thyself to venture, armed by Love.
Yet listen first what heavy trade they drive
Who would win back their dead to human arms."
So much the God; but swift, with eager eyes

And panting bosom and glorious flushed face,
The lover: "O great Love! O beautiful Love!
But if by strength is possible, of body
Or mind, battle or spirit or moving speech,
Sweet speech that makes even cruelty grow kind,
Or yearning melody—for I have heard
That when Saruswathi in heaven her harp
Has smitten, the cruel sweetness terrible
Coils taking no denial through the soul,
And tears burst from the hearts of Gods—then I,
Making great music, or with perfect words,
Will strive, or staying him with desperate hands
Match human strength 'gainst formidable Death.
But if with price, ah God! what easier! Tears
Dreadful, innumerable I will absolve,
Or pay with anguish through the centuries,
Soul's agony and torture physical,
So her small hands about my face at last
I feel, close real hair sting me with life,
And palpable breathing bosom on me press."
Then with a lenient smile the mighty God:
"O ignorant fond lover, not with tears
Shalt thou persuade immitigable Death.
He will not pity all thy pangs: nor know
His stony eyes with music to grow kind,
Nor lovely words accepts. And how wilt thou
Wrestle with that grim shadow, who canst not save
One bloom from fading? A sole thing the Gods
Demand from all men living, sacrifice:
Nor without this shall any crown be grasped.
Yet many sacrifices are there, oxen,
And prayers, and Soma wine, and pious flowers,

Blood and the fierce expense of mind, and pure
Incense of perfect actions, perfect thoughts,
Or liberality wide as the sun's,
Or ruthless labour or disastrous tears,
Exile or death or pain more hard than death,
Absence, a desert, from the faces loved;
Even sin may be a sumptuous sacrifice
Acceptable for unholy fruits. But none
Of these the inexorable shadow asks:
Alone of gods Death loves not gifts: he visits
The pure heart as the stained. Lo, the just man
Bowed helpless over his dead, nor all his virtues
Shall quicken that cold bosom: near him the wild
Marred face and passionate and will not leave
Kissing dead lips that shall not chide him more.
Life the pale ghost requires: with half thy life
Thou mayst protract the thread too early cut
Of that delightful spirit—half sweet life.
O Ruru, lo, thy frail precarious days,
And yet how sweet they are! simply to breathe
How warm and sweet! And ordinary things
How exquisite, thou then shalt learn when lost,
How luminous the daylight was, mere sleep
How soft and friendly clasping tired limbs,
And the deliciousness of common food.
And things indifferent thou then shalt want,
Regret rejected beauty, brightnesses
Bestowed in vain. Wilt thou yield up, O lover,
Half thy sweet portion of this light and gladness,
Thy little insufficient share, and vainly
Give to another? She is not thyself:
Thou dost not feel the gladness in her bosom,

Nor with the torture of thy body will she
Throb and cry out: at most with tender looks
And pitiful attempt to feel move near thee,
And weep how far she is from what she loves.
Men live like stars that see each other in heaven,
But one knows not the pleasure and the grief
The others feel: he lonely rapture has,
Or bears his incommunicable pain.
O Ruru, there are many beautiful faces,
But one thyself. Think then how thou shalt mourn
When thou hast shortened joy and feelst at last
The shadow that thou hadst for such sweet store."
He ceased with a strange doubtful look. But swift
Came back the lover's voice, like passionate rain.
"O idle words! For what is mere sunlight?
Who would live on into extreme old age,
Burden the impatient world, a weary old man,
And look back on a selfish time ill-spent
Exacting out of prodigal great life
Small separate pleasures like an usurer,
And no rich sacrifice and no large act
Finding oneself in others, nor the sweet
Expense of Nature in her passionate gusts
Of love and giving, first of the soul's needs?
Who is so coldly wise, and does not feel
How wasted were our grandiose human days
In prudent personal unshared delights?
Why dost thou mock me, friend of all the stars?
How canst thou be love's god and know not this,
That love burns down the body's barriers cold
And laughs at difference—playing with it merely
To make joy sweeter? O too deeply I know,

The lover is not different from the loved,
Nor is their silence dumb to each other. He
Contains her heart and feels her body in his,
He flushes with her heat, chills with her cold.
And when she dies, oh! when she dies, oh me,
The emptiness, the maim! the life no life,
The sweet and passionate oneness lost! And if
By shortening of great grief won back, O price
Easy! O glad briefness, aeons may envy!
For we shall live not fearing death, nor feel
As others yearning over the loved at night
When the lamp flickers, sudden chills of dread
Terrible; nor at short absence agonise,
Wrestling with mad imagination. Us
Serenely when the darkening shadow comes,
One common sob shall end and soul clasp soul,
Leaving the body in a long dim kiss.
Then in the joys of heaven we shall consort,
Amid the gladness often touching hands
To make bliss sure; or in the ghastly stream
If we must anguish, yet it shall not part
Our passionate limbs inextricably locked
By one strong agony, but we shall feel
Hell's pain half joy through sweet companionship.
God Love, I weary of words. O wing me rather
To her, my eloquent princess of the spring,
In whatsoever wintry shores she roam."
He ceased with eager forward eyes; once more
A light of beauty immortal through the limbs
Gleaming of the boy-god and soft sweet face,
Glorifying him, flushed, and he replied:
"Go then, O thou dear youth, and bear this flower

In thy hand warily. For thou shalt come
To that high meeting of the Ganges pure
With vague and violent Ocean. There arise
And loudly appeal my brother, the wild sea."
He spoke and stretched out his immortal hand,
And Ruru's met it. All his young limbs yearned
With dreadful rapture shuddering through them. He
Felt in his fingers subtle uncertain bloom,
A quivering magnificence, half fire,
Whose petals changed like flame, and from them breathed
Dangerous attraction and alarmed delight,
As at a peril near. He raised his eyes,
But the green place was empty of the God.
Only the faery tree looked up at heaven
Through branches, and with recent pleasure shook.
Then over fading earth the night was lord.

    But from Shatudru and Bipasha, streams
Once holy, and loved Iravathi and swift
Clear Chandrabhaga and Bitosta's toil
For man, went Ruru to bright sumptuous lands
By Aryan fathers not yet paced, but wild,
But virgin to our fruitful human toil,
Where nature lay reclined in dumb delight
Alone with woodlands and the voiceless hills.
He with the widening yellow Ganges came,
Amazed, to trackless countries where few tribes,
Kirath and Poundrian, warred, worshipping trees
And the great serpent. But robust wild earth,
But forests with their splendid life of beasts
Savage mastered those strong inhabitants.
Thither came Ruru. In a thin soft eve

Ganges spread far her multitudinous waves,
A glimmering restlessness with voices large,
And from the forests of that half-seen bank
A boat came heaving over it, white-winged,
With a sole silent helmsman marble-pale.
Then Ruru by his side stepped in; they went
Down the mysterious river and beheld
The great banks widen out of sight. The world
Was water and the skies to water plunged.
All night with a dim motion gliding down
He felt the dark against his eyelids; felt,
As in a dream more real than daylight,
The helmsman with his dumb and marble face
Near him and moving wideness all around,
And that continual gliding dimly on,
As one who on a shoreless water sails
For ever to a port he shall not win.
But when the darkness paled, he heard a moan
Of mightier waves and had the wide great sense
Of ocean and the depths below our feet.
But the boat stopped; the pilot lifted on him
His marble gaze cheval with the stars.
Then in the white-winged boat the boy arose
And saw around him the vast sea all grey
And heaving in the pallid dawning light.
Loud Ruru cried across the murmur: "Hear me,
O inarticulate grey Ocean, hear.
If any cadence in thy infinite
Rumour was caught from lover's moan, O Sea,
Open thy abysses to my mortal tread.
For I would travel to the despairing shades,
The spheres of suffering where entangled dwell

Souls unreleased and the untimely dead
Who weep remembering. Thither, O guide me,
No despicable wayfarer, but Ruru,
But son of a great Rishi, from all men
On earth selected for peculiar pangs,
Special disaster. Lo, this petalled fire,
How freshly it blooms and lasts with my great pain!"
He held the flower out subtly glimmering.
And like a living thing the huge sea trembled,
Then rose, calling, and filled the sight with eaves,
Converging all its giant crests; towards him
Innumerable waters loomed and heaven
Threatened. Horizon on horizon moved
Dreadfully swift; then with a prone wide sound
All Ocean hollowing drew him swiftly in,
Curving with monstrous menace over him.
He down the gulf where the loud waves collapsed
Descending, saw with floating hair arise
The daughters of the sea in pale green light,
A million mystic breasts suddenly bare,
And came beneath the flood and stunned beheld
A mute stupendous march of waters race
To reach some viewless pit beneath the world.
Ganges he saw, as men predestined rush
Upon a fearful doom foreseen, so ran,
Alarmed, with anguished speed, the river vast.
Veiled to his eyes the triple goddess rose.
She with a sound of water cried to him,
A thousand voices moaning with one pain:
"Lover, who fearedst not sunlight to leave,
With me thou mayst behold that helpless spirit
Lost in the gloom, if still thy burning bosom

Have courage to endure great Nature's night
In the dire lands where I, a goddess, mourn
Hurting my heart with my own cruelty."
She darkened to the ominous descent,
Unwilling, and her once so human waves
Sent forth a cry not meant for living ears.
And Ruru chilled; but terrible strong love
Was like a fiery finger in his breast
Pointing him on; so he through horror went
Conducted by inexorable sound.
For monstrous voices to his ear were close,
And bodiless terrors with their dimness seized him
In an obscurity phantasmal. Thus
With agony of soul to the grey waste
He came, glad of the pain of passage over,
As men who through the storms of anguish strive
Into abiding tranquil dreariness
And draw sad breath assured; to the grey waste,
Hopeless Patal, the immutable
Country, where neither sun nor rain arrives,
Nor happy labour of the human plough
Fruitfully turns the soil, but in vague sands
And indeterminable strange rocks and caverns
That into silent blackness huge recede,
Dwell the great serpent and his hosts, writhed forms,
Sinuous, abhorred, through many horrible leagues
Coiling in a half darkness. Shapes he saw,
And heard the hiss and knew the lambent light
Loathsome, but passed compelling his strong soul.
At last through those six tired hopeless worlds,
Too hopeless far for grief, pale he arrived
Into a nether air by anguish moved,

And heard before him cries that pierced the heart,
Human, not to be borne, and issued shaken
By the great river accursed. Maddened it ran,
Anguished, importunate, and in its waves
The drifting ghosts their agony endured.
There Ruru saw pale faces float of kings
And grandiose victors and revered high priests
And famous women. Now rose from the wave
A golden shuddering arm and now a face.
Torn piteous sides were seen and breasts that quailed.
Over them moaned the penal waters on,
And had no joy of their fierce cruelty.
Then Ruru, his young cheeks with pity wan,
Half moaned: "O miserable race of men,
With violent and passionate souls you come
Foredoomed upon the earth and live brief days
In fear and anguish, catching at stray beams
Of sunlight, little fragrances of flowers,
Then from your spacious earth in a great horror
Descend into this night, and here too soon
Must expiate your few inadequate joys.
O bargain hard! Death helps us not. He leads
Alarmed, all shivering from his chill embrace,
The naked spirit here. Oh my sweet flower,
Art thou too whelmed in this fierce wailing flood?
Ah me! But I will haste and deeply plunge
Into its hopeless pools and either bring
Thy old warm beauty back beneath the stars,
Or find thee out and clasp thy tortured bosom
And kiss thy sweet wrung lips and hush thy cries.
Love shall draw half thy pain into my limbs;
Then we shall triumph glad of agony."

He ceased and one replied close by his ear:
"O thou who troublest with thy living eyes
Established death, pass on. She whom thou seekest
Rolls not in the accursèd tide. For late
I saw her mid those pale inhabitants
Whom bodily anguish visits not, but thoughts
Sorrowful and dumb memories absolve,
And martyrdom of scourged hearts quivering."
He turned and saw astride the dolorous flood
A mighty bridge paved with mosaic fire,
All restless, and a woman clothed in flame,
With hands calamitous that held a sword,
Stood of the quaking passage sentinel.
Magnificent and dire her burning face.
"Pass on," she said once more, "O Bhrigu's son;
The flower protects thee from my hands." She stretched
One arm towards him and with violence
Majestic over the horrid arch compelled.
Unhurt, though shaking from her touch, alone
He stood upon an inner bank with strange
Black dreary mosses covered and perceived
A dim and level plain without one flower.
Over it paced a multitude immense
With gentle faces occupied by pain;
Strong men were there and grieving mothers, girls
With early beauty in their limbs and young
Sad children of their childlike faces robbed.
Naked they paced with falling hair and gaze
Drooping upon their bosoms, weak as flowers
That die for want of rain unmurmuring.
Always a silence was upon the place.
But Ruru came among them. Suddenly

One felt him there and looked, then as a wind
Moves over a still field of patient corn,
And the ears stir and shudder and look up
And bend innumerably flowing, so
All those dumb spirits stirred and through them passed
One shuddering motion of raised faces; then
They streamed towards him without sound and caught
With desperate hands his robe or touched his hair
Or strove to feel upon them living breath.
Pale girls and quiet children came and knelt
And with large sorrowful eyes into his looked.
Yet with their silent passion the cold hush
Moved not; but Ruru's human heart half burst
With burden of so many sorrows; tears
Welled from him; he with anguish understood
That terrible and wordless sympathy
Of dead souls for the living. Then he turned
His eyes and scanned their lovely faces strange
For that one face and found it not. He paled,
And spoke vain words into the listless air:
"O spirits once joyous, miserable race,
Happier if the old gladness were forgot!
My soul yearns with your sorrow. Yet ah! reveal
If dwell my love in your sad nation lost.
Well may you know her, O wan beautiful spirits!
But she most beautiful of all that died,
By sweetness recognisable. Her name
The sunshine knew." Speaking his tears made way:
But they with dumb lips only looked at him,
A vague and empty mourning in their eyes.
He murmured low: "Ah, folly! were she here,
Would she not first have felt me, first have raised

Her lids and run to me, leaned back her face
Of silent sorrow on my breast and looked
With the old altered eyes into my own
And striven to make my anguish understand?
Oh joy, had she been here! for though her lips
Of their old excellent music quite were robbed,
Yet her dumb passion would have spoken to me;
We should have understood each other and walked
Silently hand in hand, almost content."
He said and passed through those untimely dead.
Speechless they followed him with clinging eyes.
Then to a solemn building weird he came
With grave colossal pillars round. One dome
Roofed the whole brooding edifice, like cloud,
And at the door strange shapes were pacing, armed.
Then from their fear the sweet and mournful dead
Drew back, returning to their wordless grief.
But Ruru to the perilous doorway strode,
And those disastrous shapes upon him raised
Their bows and aimed; but he held out Love's flower,
And with stern faces checked they let him pass.
He entered and beheld a silent hall
Dim and unbounded; moving then like one
Who up a dismal stair seeks ever light,
Attained a dais brilliant doubtfully
With flaming pediment and round it coiled
Python and Naga monstrous, Joruthcaru,
Tuxuc and Vasuki himself, immense,
Magic Carcotaca all flecked with fire;
And many other prone destroying shapes
Coiled. On the wondrous dais rose a throne,
And he its pedestal whose lotus hood

With ominous beauty crowns his horrible
Sleek folds, great Mahapudma; high displayed
He bears the throne of Death. There sat supreme
With those compassionate and lethal eyes,
Who many names, who many natures holds;
Yama, the strong pure Hades sad and subtle,
Dharma, who keeps the laws of old untouched,
Critanta, who ends all things and at last
Himself shall end. On either side of him
The four-eyed dogs mysterious rested prone,
Watchful, with huge heads on their paws advanced;
And emanations of the godhead dim
Moved near him, shadowy or serpentine,
Vast Time and cold irreparable Death.
Then Ruru came and bowed before the throne;
And swaying all those figures stirred as shapes
Upon a tapestry moved by the wind,
And the sad voice was heard: "What breathing man
Bows at the throne of Hades? By what force,
Spiritual or communicated, troubles
His living beauty the dead grace of Hell?"
And one replied who seemed a neighbouring voice:
"He has the blood of Gods and Titans old.
An Apsara his mother liquid-orbed
Bore to the youthful Chyavan's strong embrace
This passionate face of earth with Eden touched.
Chyavan was Bhrigu's child, Puloma bore,
The Titaness,—Bhrigu, great Brahma's son.
Love gave the flower that helps by anguish; therefore
He chilled not with the breath of Hades, nor
The cry of the infernal stream made stone."
But at the name of Love all hell was moved.

Death's throne half faded into twilight; hissed
The phantoms serpentine as if in pain,
And the dogs raised their dreadful heads. Then spoke
Yama: "And what needs Love in this pale realm,
The warm great Love? All worlds his breath confounds,
Mars solemn order and old steadfastness.
But not in hell his legates come and go;
His vernal jurisdiction to bare Hell
Extends not. This last world resists his power
Youthful, anarchic. Here will he enlarge
Tumult and wanton joys?" The voice replied:
"Menaca momentary on the earth,
Heaven's Apsara by the fleeting hours beguiled
Played in the happy hidden glens; there bowed
To yoke of swift terrestrial joys she bore,
Immortal, to that fair Gundhurva king
A mortal blossom of delight. That bloom
Young Ruru found and plucked, but her too soon
Thy fatal hooded snake on earth surprised,
And he through gloom now travels armed by Love."
But then all Hades swaying towards him cried:
"O mortal, O misled! But sacrifice
Is stronger, nor may law of Hell or Heaven
Its fierce effectual action supersede.
Thy dead I yield. Yet thou bethink thee, mortal,
Not as a tedious evil nor to be
Lightly rejected gave the gods old age,
But tranquil, but august, but making easy
The steep ascent to God. Therefore must Time
Still batter down the glory and form of youth
And animal magnificent strong ease,
To warn the earthward man that he is spirit

Dallying with transience, nor by death he ends,
Nor to the dumb warm mother's arms is bound,
But called unborn into the unborn skies.
For body fades with the increasing soul
And wideness of its limit grown intolerant
Replaces life's impetuous joys by peace.
Youth, manhood, ripeness, age, four seasons
Twixt its return and pale departing life
Describes, O mortal,—youth that forward bends
Midst hopes, delights and dreamings; manhood deepens
To passions, toils and thoughts profound; but ripeness
For large reflective gathering-up of these,
As on a lonely slope whence men look back
Down towards the cities and the human fields
Where they too worked and laughed and loved; next age,
Wonderful age with those approaching skies.
That boon wilt thou renounce? Wherefore? To bring
For a few years—how miserably few!—
Her sunward who must after all return.
Ah, son of Rishis, cease, Lo, I remit
Hell's grasp, not oft-relinquished, and send back
Thy beautiful life unborrowed to the stars.
Or thou must render to the immutable
Total all thy fruit-bearing years; then she
Reblossoms." But the Shadow antagonist:
"Let him be shown the glory he would renounce."
And over the flaming pediment there moved,
As on a frieze a march of sculptures, carved
By Phidias for the Virgin strong and pure,
Most perfect once of all things seen in earth
Or Heaven, in Athens on the Acropolis,
But now dismembered, now disrupt! or as

In Buddhist cavern or Orissan temple,
Large aspirations architectural,
Warrior and dancing-girl, adept and king,
And conquering pomps and daily peaceful groups
Dream delicately on, softening with beauty
Great Bhuvanayshwar, the Almighty's house,
With sculptural suggestion so were limned
Scenes future on a pediment of fire.
There Ruru saw himself divine with age,
A Rishi to whom infinity is close,
Rejoicing in some green song-haunted glade
Or boundless mountain-top where most we feel
Wideness, not by small happy things disturbed.
Around him, as around an ancient tree
Its seedlings, forms august or flame-like rose;
They grew beneath his hands and were his work;
Great kings were there whom time remembers, fertile
Deep minds and poets with their chanting lips
Whose words were seed of vast philosophies
These worshipped; above this earth's half-day he saw
Amazed the dawn of that mysterious Face
And all the universe in beauty merge.
Mad the boy thrilled upwards, then spent ebbed back.
Over his mind, as birds across the sky
Sweep and are gone, the vision of those fields
And drooping faces came; almost he heard
The burdened river with human anguish wail.
Then with a sudden fury gathering
His soul he hurled out of it half its life,
And fell, like lightning, prone. Triumphant rose
The Shadow chill and deepened giant night.
Only the dais flickered in the gloom,

And those snake-eyes of cruel fire subdued.
But suddenly a bloom, a fragrance. Hell
Shuddered with bliss: resentful, overborne,
The world-besetting Terror faded back
Like one grown weak by desperate victory,
And a voice cried in Ruru's tired soul:
"Arise! the strife is over, easy now
The horror that thou hast to face, the burden
Now shared." And with a sudden burst like spring
Life woke in the strong lover over-tired.
He rose and left dim Death. Twelve times he crossed
Boithorini, the river dolorous,
Twelve times resisted Hell and hurried down
Into the ominous pit where plunges black
The vast stream thundering, saw, led puissantly
From night to unimaginable night,
As men oppressed in dreams, who cannot wake,
But measure penal visions,—punishments
Whose sight pollutes, unheard-of tortures, pangs
Monstrous, intolerable mute agonies,
Twisted unmoving attitudes of pain,
Like thoughts inhuman in statuary. A fierce
And iron voicelessness had grasped those worlds.
No horror of cries expressed their endless pain,
No saving struggle, no breathings of the soul.
And in the last hell irremediable
Where Ganges clots into that fatal pool,
Appalled he saw her; pallid, listless, bare—
O other than that earthly warmth and grace
In which the happy roses deepened and dimmed
With come-and-go of swift enamoured blood!
Dumb drooped she; round her shapes of anger armed

Stood dark like thunder-clouds. But Ruru sprang
Upon them, burning with the admitted God.
They from his touch like ineffectual fears
Vanished; then sole with her, trembling he cried
The old glad name and crying bent to her
And touched, and at the touch the silent knots
Of Hell were broken and its sombre dream
Of dreadful stately pains at once dispersed.
Then as from one whom a surpassing joy
Has conquered, all the bright surrounding world
Streams swiftly into distance, and he feels
His daily senses slipping from his grasp,
So that unbearable enormous world
Went rolling mighty shades, like the wet mist
From men on mountain-tops; and sleep outstretched
Rising its soft arms towards him and his thoughts,
As on a bed, sank to ascending void.

    But when he woke, he heard the koïl insist
On sweetness and the voice of happy things
Content with sunlight. The warm sense was round him
Of old essential earth, known hues and custom
Familiar tranquillising body and mind,
As in its natural wave a lotus feels.
He looked and saw all grass and dense green trees,
And sunshine and a single grasshopper
Near him repeated fierily its note.
Thrilling he felt beneath his bosom her;
Oh, warm and breathing were those rescued limbs
Against the greenness, vivid, palpable, white,
With great black hair and real and her cheek's
Old softness and her mouth a dewy rose.

For many moments comforting his soul
With all her jasmine body sun-ensnared
He fed his longing eyes and, half in doubt,
With touches satisfied himself of her.
Hesitating he kissed her eyelids. Sighing
With a slight sob she woke and earthly large
Her eyes looked upward into his. She stretched
Her arms up, yearning, and their souls embraced;
Then twixt brief sobbing laughter and blissful tears,
Clinging with all her limbs to him, "O love,
The green green world! the warm sunlight!" and ceased,
Finding no words; but the earth breathed round them,
Glad of her children and the koïl's voice
Persisted in the morning of the world.

www.ingramcontent.com/pod-product-compliance
Lightning Source LLC
LaVergne TN
LVHW041502070426
835507LV00009B/761